The New Novello Choral Edition
NOVELLO HANDEL EDITION

General Editor   Donald Burrows

T0056686

TE DEUM in A MAJOR
(HWV 282)

for ATB soloists, SATB chorus and orchestra

Edited by Donald Burrows

Vocal Score

NOVELLO PUBLISHING LIMITED
14 - 15 Berners Street, London, W1T 3LJ

© 2011 Novello & Company Limited

Published in Great Britain by Novello Publishing Limited
Head office: 14 - 15 Berners Street, London W1T 3LJ
Tel +44 (0)207 612 7400   Fax +44 (0)207 612 7545

Sales and Hire: Music Sales Distribution Centre
Newmarket Road, Bury St Edmunds, Suffolk, IP33 3YB
Tel +44 (0)1284 702600   Fax +44 (0)1284 768301

Web: www.musicroom.com   www.chesternovello.com

All rights reserved   Printed in Great Britain

CONTENTS

Approximate duration
17 minutes

INSTRUMENTATION

Flute
Oboe
Bassoon
Strings
Continuo (Harpsichord or Organ)

The performing material for this edition
includes a fully-realised Continuo part.

PREFACE

On 25 February 1723 a warrant was issued from the Lord Chamberlain of the British court for the admission of Handel into the 'Place and Quality of Composer of Musick for his Majesty's Chappel Royal'. Although this was accompanied by a generous additional pension and carried a title comparable to a German *Kapellmeister*, the appointment was largely honorary and did not involve Handel in the daily routine of services. He did, however, have to fulfil one occasional duty by providing special music for the Sunday morning services in the Chapel Royal, St James's Palace, following King George I's return from visits to his Electorate in Hanover.[1] During the remainder of the King's reign there were just two such events, in January 1724 and January 1726, and the first of them was reported as follows in the London newspapers:

> Yesterday being the First Sunday after his Majesty's safe Arrival at St. James's, *Te Deum* and a fine New Anthem composed by the famous M. Handel, were performed both vocally and instrumentally at the Royal Chapel there by the greatest masters, before his Majesty and their Royal Highnesses.

The musical items were performed within the Anglican liturgy of Morning Prayer from the *Book of Common Prayer*, in which the Te Deum was one of the regular canticles and provision was made for the inclusion of an anthem. In all, Handel composed five settings of the English Te Deum text, and they vary in scale according to the events for which they were intended. The longest and grandest were composed for public occasions: the Utrecht Peace celebrations in 1713 and the Dettingen victory in 1743 (though, as it happened, the latter did not in the event receive a big public thanksgiving service). Another extended setting was composed during Handel's period of association with James Brydges's private group of musicians at Cannons, and was a companion to the 'Chandos' anthems. The other two were composed for various Chapel Royal services and are more modest in scope, partly on account of limitations imposed by the size of the King's private chapel and by the court timetable that required the Sunday morning service to be over in time for the King to dine 'in public'. The A major Te Deum is the most intimate, and perhaps the most personal, of Handel's five settings of the text: although it has moments of grandeur, it also has a chamber-scale sensitivity in the scoring and the use of the solo voices. Its compact treatment of the varying moods in the words provides vivid contrasts, including an unusual drift into the key of F sharp minor at the mention of 'the Holy Ghost, the Comforter', which is then brought back down to earth by the D major of the succeeding movement. For some sections of the Te Deum, Handel drew upon musical ideas from his Cannons setting (and, to a lesser extent, from a previous Chapel Royal work), but the working-out and balance of the material was thoroughly reconsidered. Furthermore, even literal musical borrowings were enhanced in various ways: the opening to No 6, for example, adds a bassoon obbligato in duet with the oboe solo derived from the Cannons version.

The original vocal performers for the A major Te Deum would have been the regular members of the Chapel Royal choir, probably no more than eight boys and a dozen men who were 'in waiting' at the time. From within the choir, Handel featured the leading voices of the alto Francis Hughes and the bass Samuel Weely as soloists: there was also a more modest solo role for the tenor Thomas Gethin. He also made good use of musical interactions between the soloists and their colleagues to enrich and enliven the texture of chorus movements. The core of the accompaniment was provided by about a dozen string players from the King's Musicians, supplemented by some additional instrumentalists who were brought in specially. Payments in court documents record the employment of two double bass players (instruments which were not covered from the regular Musicians), the oboe player John Kytch and a bassoon player; most likely, Handel directed the performances from the organ. It is not certain whether the year for the performance of the A major Te Deum was 1724 or 1726, though the latter is slightly more likely. The bassoonists were Richard Vincent in 1724 and Godfried Karpa in 1726: whichever of them was involved must have been an outstanding player, for the Te Deum and its companion anthem (*Let God arise*, HWV 256b) contain the most interesting and extensive obbligato music that Handel ever wrote for the instrument. The anthem is also published in the Novello Handel Edition and the two works can be programmed together effectively.

SOME PRACTICAL CONSIDERATIONS

Although practical necessity has required presentation of the Te Deum in eight movements, it is clear that Handel regarded some sequences of these movements as connected. Nos 5 and 7 are independent aria-style movements, and the long-note ending to No 6 clearly indicates the conclusion of a section; elsewhere, however, both musical and verbal sense require continuity between movements. Nos 1-3 thus form one larger unit, and No 4, with its dominant-chord ending, serves as an introduction to No 5.

RHYTHMIC ALTERATION

Editorial suggestions for rhythmic modifications, indicated by 'flags' above the notes, have been added to cover two contexts: places where the last note of a phrase needs to be shortened in order to clear a harmonic change or a solo entry, and places where a rhythm may be amended to conform to the movement of other parts or the prevailing pattern. Handel's notation is presented as the music text except at the following places in No 1: bar 9 beat 2 (Alto solo and Alto chorus), Bar 10 beat 4 (Alto and Bass solo), bar 14 beat 2 (Alto and Tenor chorus), bar 15 beat 4 (Soprano chorus and Alto solo). Here he wrote even-semiquaver groups, but there is a good case for synchronisation with other vocal and instrumental parts and the provision of the necessary flags would be intrusive.

MATTERS FOR SINGERS

The principal solo parts are for one alto and one bass; the brief solo passages for tenor (No 2, No 3 bars 28-31, No 6 bars 27-30) may be taken by a member of the chorus. Handel wrote a stave for a second bass soloist (Bernard Gates) in the chorus movements, but the music of this part basically comprises variants on the chorus bass in Nos 1, 3, 4, 6 (bar 56 onwards) and 8 (final chord). The 'Bass 2' part is shown as an upper variant on the Bass Chorus stave, and can be taken either by a soloist or a few voices, as suits circumstances with regard to the balance of parts. In many places the musical role of the alto and bass soloists in chorus movements is to strengthen the next-highest part. The alto parts (solo and chorus) can be taken by suitable male or female voices. Handel wrote alternative melodic lines for the alto soloist at No 7 bars 25-6, though only the lower version appears in secondary copies.

CONTINUO ACCOMPANIMENT

As is apparent from the music printed as small-size notes in the right-hand part of the accompaniment to this vocal score, some passages are accompanied by the basso continuo only, without upper orchestral instruments, though these passages are less extensive than in the airs from Handel's operas and oratorios. At the Chapel Royal the chord-playing continuo function for this work was performed by Handel on the organ, possibly a chamber organ brought in for the occasion rather than the Chapel's resident instrument. (This was the only chord-playing instrument involved, in contrast to his practice in theatre oratorios, where both harpsichord and organ were employed.) The Chapel Royal staff included a Lutenist, but the person concerned also had a place in the Musicians and would have performed in the string-orchestra ensemble instead. The basso continuo obviously requires the participation of at least one chord-playing instrument. A fully-realised continuo part is included with the performing material of this edition, suitable for organ or harpsichord in present-day performances. The realisation follows the figuring from Handel's bass part, but this is very sporadic and the best guide lies in the harmonic implications of the music itself. A reduction in bassi instruments, to a continuo group of cello and organ (possibly with double bass), for passages accompanied by continuo alone, may not be necessary if modest instrumental forces are involved; editorial suggestions are, however, provided for this possibility when a larger orchestra is involved. This matter is discussed further in the Preface to the full score.

THE KEYBOARD ACCOMPANIMENT

Abbreviations at the beginning of each movement indicate the scoring: these are provided to assist the planning of rehearsals. The only variation in the scoring involves a flute instead of an oboe in No 5; Bsn* indicates that the Bassoon part for the movement concerned is editorial (i.e. not specified in source **A**, though supported by **F**).

The keyboard accompaniment is a practical reduction of the principal activity in the orchestral parts, suitable for rehearsal accompaniment. The harmonic bass line is preserved as the lowest part. This presents some practical problems on account of the interweaving of the Bassoon part with the Bassi in No 5 bars 26-28 and throughout No 7. If piano accompaniment is used it is effective just to play the full-sized notes shown in the left-hand stave (taken principally from the Bassoon part); with organ accompaniment the Bassi part, shown as small-sized notes, may be incorporated with the pedals. Bassoon obbligato passages are a particular feature of this work, but in some places (especially in No 2) it has been impossible to incorporate them into the accompaniment.

'Senza DB.' indicates orchestral passages without double bass, and 'Bassi' indicates subsequent re-entries; 'Cont.' indicates passages accompanied by the Continuo, including those where Handel's bass line shows the doubling of upper parts (usually chorus entries) without the participation of orchestral bass instruments. Editorial continuo realisation, shown in small-size notes, has taken account of Handel's intermittent continuo figurings. Indications for trills (from the sources, and editorial suggestions) are included, but all may not be practical for the keyboard accompaniment; in many places Handel's standard 'tr' marking indicates a short ornament.

SOURCES
i) HANDEL'S AUTOGRAPH SCORE
A London, British Library, RM 20.g.4, ff. 1-20. Handel's autograph is undated but concludes with the inscription 'S[oli] D[eo] G[loria]'. The autograph of the companion anthem HWV 256b is now bound in the same volume, and the two have many features in common, including the same type of manuscript paper, similar orchestral scorings and the same named solo singers. The end of the anthem autograph is lost, and this may originally have carried Handel's completion date for the composition of the two works. The autograph of the Te Deum is complete apart from one apparently anomalous feature. No 2 is missing, but was indicated by Handel with the cue 'To the [sic] all angels from the other score'. The construction of the paper-gatherings leaves no possibility that pages have been lost at this point; neither the autograph of the movement nor the 'other score' survive. While it seems possible that Handel accidentally omitted to set the text of No 2 when he initially wrote the autograph, it is also unlikely that he ever intended the final chord of No 1 to be followed by the opening of No 3. Bassoon staves, in the Te Deum and its companion anthem, are consistently labelled 'Basson', but Handel's cues at No 6 bars 54 and 56 refer to 'Bassons'.

ii) MANUSCRIPT COPIES
B Manchester Public Library, Henry Watson Music Library, MS 130 Hd4 v.47(1). Full score, in a volume with the Chapel Royal anthems HWV 256b and 250b, copied by an unknown scribe, *c.* 1725-30. Unlike many other Handel items now at Manchester, this volume apparently did not originate from the 'Aylesford Collection'.
The copy was derived from the autograph; it includes the names of the original singers and No 2.

C London, Royal College of Music MS 1057. Full score, originally paginated 1-58, bound into a volume of miscellaneous manuscripts that was probably assembled by John Alcock in the 1760s. The Te Deum was copied *c.*1725-30, possibly by someone with Chapel Royal connections; it includes the singers' names and the music for No 2.

D Bethlehem, Pennsylvania, U.S.A., Moravian Archives L-MISC-13. Full score, *c.* 1735-40, by an unidentified copyist, with German text added in red ink. It includes No 2 but no singers' names.

E Danish private collection. Full score volume with the Te Deum (pages 1-59) and two anthems. Copied *c.* 1735 by S3.[2] It includes No 2 but no singers' names; the music text is good, but it contains some additional tempo indications (listed below, under 'Textual Notes') of doubtful authenticity. London, Guildhall Library, Gresham Music Library MSS 365, 366 are part-books for oboe/flute and bassoon, also copied by S3, which were probably derived from, and contemporary with, this score.

F Henry Watson Music Library, MS 130 Hd4 v.325 (score) and associated part-books, vocal and instrumental, in vv.327-335, 338-47. From the 'Aylesford Collection', originally copied by S2 for Charles Jennens, the score *c.* 1740 and the part-books about five years later. Derived from the autograph: the score has Handel's cue for No 2 but not the music, and the part-books have blank staves for this movement. The copyist prepared the part-books according to current oratorio practice and without knowledge of the circumstances of the original performance: there are duplicate parts for Oboes and Bassoons (Bassoon 2 having the continuo bass line in some movements where Bassoon 1 has an obbligato part), though it is clear that there were only single players for Oboe and Bassoon at the Chapel Royal. The Oboe part-books also contain the music for flute; this accords with eighteenth-century practice, but does not necessarily mean that both instruments were taken by the same player.

G Royal College of Music MS 890. Full score in the hand of Edmund Thomas Warren, copied *c.* 1760, formerly in the library of the Concerts of Ancient Music. It includes No 2.

Copies **B-G** have some errors but in general convey good musical texts; the following copies convey less accurate texts, and were probably derived from lost intermediate sources.

H British Library Add. MS 29998, ff.2-29 (original pagination 1-55). Full score, copied *c.* 1725-30, possibly by Thomas Barnard. The original singers' names are included.

J Oxford, Bodleian Library MS Mus.c.25, ff. 28-55 (original pagination 1-55), copyist unidentified. Full score, copied *c.* 1725-30, probably for Sir John Dolben, whose signature is on the printed edition of Purcell's D major Te Deum and Jubilate which is bound with the MS.

K London, Foundling Museum, Gerald Coke Handel Collection 1279. Full score, copied *c.* 1725-50, copyist unidentified. Bookplate of 'Messrs Sharp' from the later eighteenth century; subsequently owned by E. F. Rimbault.

L British Library R.M. 19.g.1 vol. 1, ff. 123-156 (original pagination 1-67). Full score, from the 'Smith Collection' copied *c.* 1765 by S11.

M Foundling Museum, Coke Collection 1242. Full score dated 1766-7, copyist unidentified.

N New Brunswick (New Jersey, U.S.A.), Rutgers, M2038.H14A5, vol. 2 (appendix), pp. 1-61. Full score, copied *c.* 1770 by S10, probably for Sir William Watkins Wynn.

O Foundling Museum, Coke Collection 1258. Full score, unidentified copyist, bound with a score of the anthem HWV 256b, dated 1770.

iii) PRINTED EDITIONS

Ar *Te Deum in Score Composed for His Grace the Duke of Chandos (in the Year 1720) By G. F. Handel* Samuel Arnold's edition, fascicle No XX (1788). The music text was derived from a manuscript in the **H-O** group; the description on the title-page is clearly erroneous.

HG *Te Deum I* in a volume of three Te Deum settings, Händelgesellschaft Edition vol. 37 (1872), pp. 109-138, edited by Friedrich Chrysander.

EDITORIAL PRACTICE

The main source for this edition is **A**, Handel's autograph; the music text for No 2 is provided by copies **B-D**. The Bassoon part-books from **F** confirm the role of that instrument on the bassi line in the movements and passages where Handel did not write a separate stave or cue for the bassoon. All other copies have been checked in detail but make no significant additional contribution. The principal sources provide an accurate and comprehensive text: the few points requiring editorial intervention or interpretation are listed below, except for those that involve only the instrumental parts, which are dealt with in the Preface to the full score. Movement numberings are editorial.

Clefs have been modernised for the vocal parts: the original clefs were soprano (C1) for soprano voices, alto (C3) for alto voices, and tenor (C4) for tenor voices.

Handel's system for accidentals has been modernised, and small-size accidentals are used where he may have omitted an intended inflection. The conventional long notes in the final bars of Nos 6 and 8 have been retained. Handel's slurs in the vocal parts to indicate the word-setting have been omitted, and his note-beaming has been modernised. Slurs in the orchestral parts from the principal sources are included, but obvious *simile* slurs and staccato dashes are not indicated as editorial unless there is some anomaly in the pattern; in the full score all slurs that do not have authority from the principal sources are shown as editorial. The *hemiola*, or conventional cadential rhythmic re-grouping in triple time, is indicated by horizontal square brackets thus: ⌐⌐⌐⌐⌐⌐. Editorial suggestions for rhythmic modification are shown by 'flags' above the stave or stave-system: see above, 'Rhythmic Alteration'. Editorial suggestions for additional dynamics, tempo directions, staccato dashes, trills, etc. are shown in square brackets, and editorial slurs or ties are shown thus: ⌒. Where, however, Handel indicated general dynamics incompletely these have been applied to all parts without editorial indication, and the same applies to the addition of *f* at the beginnings of movements to which Handel added *piano* in subsequent bars.

TEXTUAL NOTES

All listed readings relate to source **A**, unless otherwise noted. Additional details relating only to the orchestral parts are noted in the Preface to the full score for this edition.

No. 2

Bar

1   No tempo marking in **A** or **B**; **E** has *Largo*, but it seems more appropriate to continue at the same tempo as No. 1, or slightly faster.

1-4   The distinction in the rhythm from the following bars is found in all reliable early copies, as are also the apparent inconsistencies in bars 9-11 and 14-15.

9-14   The copies, probably faithfully copying the lost autograph, combine T solo and T chorus on one stave, with some ambiguity; T solo as given here is the most likely interpretation.

No. 3

17   No tempo marking in **A**; *Andante* in **E**.

49   BSolo: last two notes f (Handel mistakenly wrote these as if in the tenor clef).

No. 4

1   *Allegro* in **E**, conflicting with Handel's tempo in **A**.

No. 6

13   Bass parts: beat 4 even quavers in B1, ambiguous in B2, dotted group in B3 (chorus) and Bassi: regularised to dotted group in **B**.

30-31   B chorus: tie in B2 (Gates solo) but not B3 (chorus).

18   No tempo marking in **A**; *Andante* in **E**.

48   S, last note: Handel wrote b′ (octaves with bass); amended to conform to d′′ in Vln 1.

No. 7

1   No tempo marking in **A**; *Largo andante* in **E**.

No. 8

16   Bassi: Handel's cue at beat 4 reads 'Violoncello. le Basson. l'organo'; this is the only mention of the organ in the autographs of the Te Deum and the contemporary anthem.

ACKNOWLEDGMENTS

I extend my grateful thanks to the owners and curators of the sources for this edition, for facilitating access to the original materials. Research for the edition, and initial preparation of the music text by Blaise Compton, was supported by the Arts Faculty at The Open University. I thank those involved in the production of this edition, in particular Howard Friend and Hywel Davies from Novello Publishing.

Donald Burrows, 2010

1   For details of Handel's association with the Chapel Royal, and the music involved, see Donald Burrows, *Handel and the English Chapel Royal* (Oxford, 2005).

2   For the 'S' classification of Handel's music copyists, see Jens Peter Larsen, *Handel's 'Messiah': Origins, Composition, Sources* (London, 1957), Chapter 4.

TE DEUM IN A MAJOR

GEORGE FRIDERIC HANDEL
HWV 282

No. 1

Soli and Chorus WE PRAISE THEE, O GOD
Chorus with Alto and Bass soli

3

No. 2 — Soli and Chorus TO THEE ALL ANGELS CRY ALOUD
Chorus with Alto, Tenor and Bass soli

No. 3   Soli and Chorus TO THEE CHERUBIM AND SERAPHIM
Chorus with Alto, Tenor and Bass soli

7

8

on - ly Son,___ al - - - so the Ho - ly Ghost, the com - fort - er.

No. 4 Chorus THOU ART THE KING OF GLORY, O CHRIST
Chorus with Alto and Bass soli

No. 5   Solo WHEN THOU TOOKEST UPON THEE TO DELIVER MAN
Alto solo

Note: in bars 26-8 large-sized notes are for piano accompaniment. Additional notes from the Bassi are shown small-sized and may be included in organ accompaniment.

womb.   When thou

had'st ov - er - come_____ the____ sharp - ness of death,

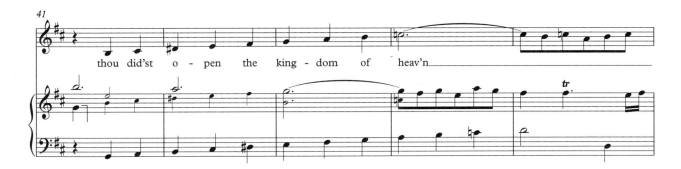

thou did'st o - pen the king - dom of heav'n_____

to all____ be - liev - ers.

Thou sit - test_____ at the

15

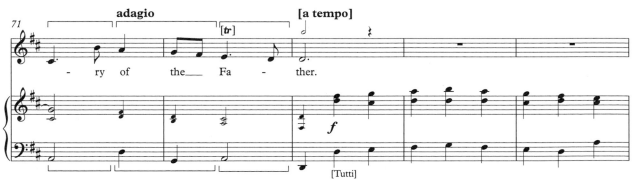

No. 6   Soli and Chorus WE BELIEVE THAT THOU SHALT COME TO BE OUR JUDGE

Chorus with Alto, Tenor and Bass soli

15

help thy ser-vants, whom thou hast re - deem'd with thy pre - cious blood.

help thy ser-vants, whom thou hast re - deem'd with thy pre - cious blood.

help thy ser-vants, whom thou hast re - deem'd with thy pre - cious blood.

help thy ser-vants, whom thou hast re - deem'd with thy pre - cious blood.

help thy ser-vants, whom thou hast re - deem'd with thy pre - cious blood.

help thy ser-vants, whom thou hast re - deem'd with thy pre - cious blood.

18 **[poco più mosso]**

Make them to be num-ber'd with_____ thy saints in glo - - - -

[poco più mosso]

p

20

No. 7   Solo   VOUCHSAFE, O LORD
Alto solo

Note: on the lower stave of the keyboard part, large-sized notes are for piano accompaniment. Additional notes from the Bassi part, shown small-sized may be included in organ accompaniment. See Preface.

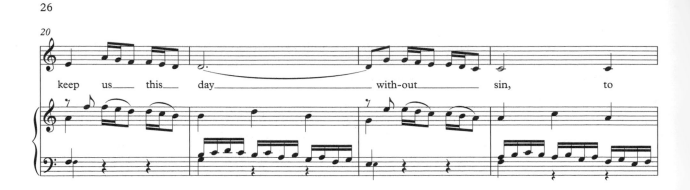

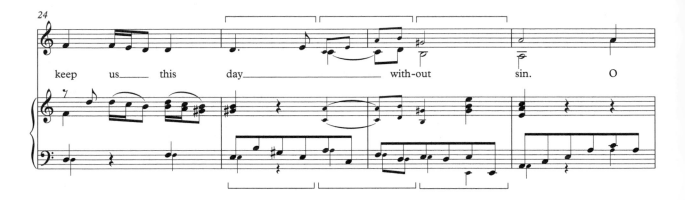

Bars 25-6, Alto Solo: Handel wrote alternative versions in **A**

up-on us; O_____ Lord, let thy

mer - cy light-en up-on us as our

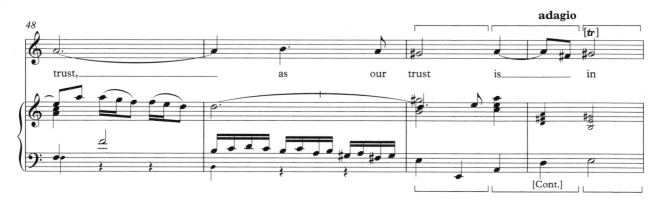

trust,_____ as our trust is_____ in

thee.

28

No. 8   Chorus O LORD, IN THEE HAVE I TRUSTED
Chorus with Alto and Bass soli

Senza D.B.

Bar 21, Soprano: Handel wrote both notes as alternatives